UNDER THE SIGN

ALSO BY ANN LAUTERBACH

Poems

Or to Begin Again

Hum

If in Time: Selected Poems 1975–2000

On a Stair

And for Example

Clamor

Before Recollection

Many Times, but Then

Prose

The Given & The Chosen

The Night Sky: Writings on the Poetics of Experience

BOOKS WITH ARTISTS

Thripsis
(with Joe Brainard)

A Clown, Some Colors, A Doll, Her Stories, A Song, A Moonlit Cover
(with Ellen Phelan)

How Things Bear Their Telling
(with Lucio Pozzi)

Greeks
(with Jan Groover and Bruce Boice)

Sacred Weather
(with Louisa Chase)

UNDER THE SIGN

ANN LAUTERBACH

PENGUIN POETS

PENGUIN BOOKS
Published by the Penguin Group
Penguin Group (USA) LLC
375 Hudson Street
New York, New York 10014

USA | Canada | UK | Ireland | Australia | New Zealand | India | South Africa | China
penguin.com
A Penguin Random House Company

First published in Penguin Books 2013

Library of Congress Cataloging-in-Publication Data
Lauterbach, Ann
[Poems. Selections]
Under the Sign / Ann Lauterbach.
pages cm. — (Penguin Poets)
Poems.
ISBN 978-0-14-312418-4
I. Title.
PS3562.A844U53   2013
811'.54—dc23   2013021794

Printed in the United States of America
1 3 5 7 9 10 8 6 4 2

Set in ITC New Baskerville Std
Designed by Ginger Legato

In memory of
Leslie Scalapino
Stacy Doris
and for our students

ACKNOWLEDGMENTS

The author gratefully acknowledges the editors of the following journals, in which some of these poems, often in earlier versions, were first published: *The Brooklyn Rail, Conjunctions, Critical Quarterly, Denver Quarterly, Maggy, Vanitas,* and *Formes Poétiques Contemporaines.*

Thanks also to Paul Slovak for patience and perseverance, and Anna Moschovakis, Marina van Zuylen, Michael Brenson, and Nancy Shaver for their enduring friendship and help along the way.

CONTENTS

I. GLYPH

A READING ■ 3

TESTING THE WATERS ■ 6

GLYPH ■ 9

THE TRANSLATOR'S DILEMMA ■ 11

ENIGMA OF THE CAT ■ 12

TRIPTYCH (VAN EYCK) ■ 18

UNTITLED (PORTRAIT) ■ 22

LANDSCAPE WITHOUT VIEW ■ 24

NIGHT NEWS WITH FAKE ZEBRA ■ 27

AFTER NEWTOWN ■ 30

UGLY SONNET ■ 31

WORLD CUP ■ 32

MEANWHILE, STORM ■ 33

IL PLEUT ■ 35

DOMESTIC MODERNISM ■ 36

UTENSIL ■ 38

HARBOR SONG ■ 40

BASEMENT TAPE ■ 41

UNDER THE SIGN ■ 43

ALICE IN OCTOBER ■ 44

THE TEARS OF EROS ■ 45

II. TASK: TO OPEN ■ 51

III. DEAR INSTRUCTOR

UNTITLED (SPOON) ■ 83

OF SPIRITS ■ 85

LETTER (IN PRAISE OF PROMISCUITY) ■ 87

UNTITLED (AGAINST PERFECTION) ■ 89

ZERO & A ■ 91

A PLAN ■ 98

UNTITLED (FATE) ■ 99

A FOLD IN TIME ■ 102

AT/OR (RAÚL ZURITA) ■ 104

UNTITLED (THE DISINHERITED) ■ 106

BEAUTY AND CONSOLATION (RICHARD RORTY) ■ 111

UNTITLED (THE RIVER) ■ 114

UNTITLED (THE NEUTRAL) ■ 120

TO THE GIVEN ■ 126

CLASSICAL AUGURY ■ 129

SOME ELEMENTS OF THE POEM ■ 131

SONG OF THE *O* (EMERSON "CIRCLES") ■ 137

People wish to be settled; only so far as they are unsettled is there any hope for them.

Ralph Waldo Emerson

I.

GLYPH

A READING

1.

Mutable stipend, junk

saturated in the moldy

room with a thin blue rug.

The pivot has some mystery

as in the dream: huge

white birds flowering down.

The morning was brilliant

but then junk

broke loose to scatter sky.

Was I meant to consult

this tissue of meaningless harbingers?

2.

Make no mistake: behind

a curtain, a continuum.

Blink, sun.

The bugs are back.

The skin is salty.

Behind the curtain, a

mistake or just old dark

thrown across space.

I have an inky drawing of a hairy

stick pressing wind.

Lovely, now, the milky shade.

Behind the curtain, junk

orbits and a serenade to

those who keep watch while the ditch

fills with lost things. The distant river

flirts with light. The water is alight.

3.

In the dust of a former

moon, an abridgment.

If this were prose, little

agreements would obtain,

and you could turn toward the missed

like an angel on a fence.

I mean a bird, a bird

in prose. The spun ordeal

arises as a missing object, its

body enclosed so to be

a convenient newsy thing,

the dead soldier's spouse.

What exactly was intended

to be kept in this regressive frame?

Some figure? Some petty marker?

She will trade her mother's

ring for passage. Let her come aboard.

Veet! Veet! The blue jay's yell

is hollow the way that light blinds.

TESTING THE WATERS

1.

What world?
asked the boy, alarmed

to be asked
to say when or

what might be repeated
the soldier's word

the doctor's word, how
world might be

known by saying.

2.

Gone now from the said

radical child

hears only an orgy of hunches

under the swollen noise.

Fair trade. Liaison. Betrayal.

Some of us, some of them,

no accounting for response

as in the screen palace

we count our dead.

Blind to this or that

futurist moment

there are so many moments untold.

Who then arranged

this episode? Who then

killed the child?

3.

I'm getting good at sailing
unaccompanied through time

holding on to delay
forfeiting

the familiar bridge
across a mirage

betrayal
whose voice concedes

and is still recalled
even as it bends

under the weight
of forgetfulness.

I'm getting good at counting
and at seeing

the view from the
window of a dream.

4.

We hunker down

under the pines

and refuse to recall.

Fire! Excellent inferno!

Another cosmos passes through.

The mild noises of night

are a form of waiting

and then the dream

touches and reminds like a hand.

This reveals, and so a weary ambit

collapses the foreground scene.

GLYPH

It was, she said, her favorite color.
Fine, I said, have it your way.

He said he loved small things.
How small? I asked. No answer.

A book arrived in the mail I did not order.
The leaves, many of them, were falling.

Perhaps, I thought, it was sent just in case.
It was, she said, her favorite color.

The dog barked. He was new to the neighborhood.
Fine, I said, have it your way.

He said he loved small things.
A book arrived in the mail I did not order.

Today was more or less full of surprises.
Something in the mix of habit and hope.

Surprise, she said, is a kind of wind.
Perhaps, I thought, it was sent just in case.

To what or to whom are you referring?
I refer, she said, to the dog.

How small? I asked. No answer.
The leaves, many of them, were falling.

The dog barked. He was new to the neighborhood.
It was, she said, her favorite color.

Do animals forget? I asked.
The leaves, many of them, were falling.

Something in the mix of habit and hope.
A book arrived in the mail I did not order.

How small? I asked. No answer.
Today was more or less full of surprises.

to Celia Bland

To foretell an ordinary mission, with fewer words.
With fewer, more ordinary, words.
Words of one syllable, for example.

For example: *step* and *sleeve.*
These are two favorites, among many.
Many can be found if I look closely.

But even if I look closely, surely a word is not
necessarily here, in the foreground.
I see an edge of a paper, I see orange.

I see words and I see things. An old story,
nothing to foretell the ordinary mission.
I see "her winter" and I see

And even the Romans fear her by now.
Are these words in
translation or barriers to translation?

I see John and an open book, open to a day
in August. I am feeling defeated
among these sights, as if I will never find

either sleeve or step. These ordinary
pleasurable words, attached to
ordinary pleasurable things, as if

to find them is to say I am
announcing criteria. *Step, sleeve,*
you are invited to come up and be within

ordinary necessities. Staircase. Coat.

1.

She walked along. She looked out.

Nothing here, among these, resembles.

She went on. There were lists,

objects, names, but still

nothing resembling. The sky

was a kind of sorrow, cold

and stained a pale sunless gray,

it too did not resemble. And she,

her lies adrift over the humdrum,

thought to turn back but by then

as you already know was lost.

2.

The wrist's illness, having
touched the spider,

erupting as grid
sewn before and after the fact.

The dark hall, the walls,
the imagined street

where the forecast
elicits a halo

broken from the entire—
cusp, turn, rim.

3.

Cat sleeps through world.

4.

Come then, undo the truss.

Mayhem waits like a sting.

Look down into the face puddle,

look across into the alarm.

There is a boat on a roof,

an image of a boat

on a roof. All else is heaved

as if giving birth on a floor.

Have you come this far?

Will you pass the wet caul?

5.

Cat is spared from angel.

6.

Mute extravagance

trapped under tarp.

Wave good-bye or

establish some rules

despite the glare.

Look down, there are things

dumped into a pail of glue.

This belt is way too tight.

These buttons, coins,

crumbs, a derelict parade

awash, happy tramp drowned.

7.

Cat plays with dead bird.

8.

You cannot avoid

the information.

No one cares what you

say unless you say

the information.

No one cares

what you care about

unless it is

the information

turned toward

a vocabulary

as if written.

9.

Cat turns in the chair and subsides.

10.

For what do you search?

The quick being

out of which

the conceptual flares

like a toy bomb.

The medieval crescent

born from prolific

reason.

Are you ready?

After the after, please

throw away

the photographs.

We know the image

came to nothing.

11.

Cat at the threshold.

12.

To dream is

to proliferate

in the opening that is

always shut. The long self

drawn into patterns of shadow,

girls and boys nameless

across the playground.

Stranded here

in the partial real. Ground

parts on

lacerations of the newly good.

The stone is mentioned.

A law is invoked.

The event floats in from afar.

13.

Cat waits until dark to go out.

TRIPTYCH (VAN EYCK)

1.

The woman

with a child on her lap
sitting on rugs

what is she doing

there
in the middle

the day
might always be cold

March light

what is she doing
sitting with a child

on her lap

long drapes
behind

and rugs
like wings

or feathers
feathery rugs

alive in the cold

March light
flat as the moon

at dusk

the cold
rakes

blue plumes

into
traversing

signals
aside

and because
it can never be

early enough
she is always

sitting
aside

in wait.

2.

Mal, mal,
trivial thwart.

Stop this
glare, stop

goading the ill
into consequence,

the extra
bloom

unheralded
by day or by night.

Go off
into a woody scene

and take
the painted epilogue

with you.
Burn it for heat

and burn the
currency of emeralds

mistaken
for new life.

3.

If *no time's*
not want

stay and
renovate

traced gloves
sweet digits

adhesives
bound for dispatch

and so cling
to the tiered ensemble

stupendous enrichment
during the spell and

start, start.

for Stacy

UNTITLED (PORTRAIT)

Up here in the ancient gold trim   the news not yet visual

so that he or she or we are invisible to the naked eye

whereas the gold trim on her gown is etched

falling down along and over to the hem

like an evening sky.

           Or like nothing yet announced

so the missing and the present are singular in their dress

as we await the address and the black

river of reading aloud over the phone

George Eliot's intervention between the walls

so that we walk through them as if turning a page

we agreed again you and I as we have agreed before

you are not going to be with me on the other side of the wall

despite George Eliot and despite Daniel

in his pink house with the book

whose cover is reiterated on the wall

the picture of the beautiful woman in black

who had to decide whether to be her portrait

or to be someone else

not like the mother or the sister

not like the man in the hotel room in his bathrobe

with his whore and his

                unspeakable

so that the only thing to be said

is *you cannot do that with me in the room*

the walls of the room and the long view across the river

where there are others in their rooms

and the house from the other side of the river

looks immense

             as the life within is immense.

LANDSCAPE WITHOUT VIEW

These intensities   their wake   the jar

fret   the word

snow on dry leaves   *fret fret*

the jar dark inside within   in the dark

body o body not that anyone is here

the thick stiff night's

curled domain

as of now   how it is spoken

the slide between

the mere passage

                    fret

and surely the blind spot

the occasion

emphatic   these intensities

not sheltered not yet drawn

by the most implicated

what it looks like

to halt   crassly halt

and the new digital figure

axiomatic grace

semblance ushered from sequence

avenue or image

sucking at the animate

these contagious exceptions

fugitive incursions

even so the turbines hum

licking at stone

the contagion of stone

peevish annunciation

melded onto a screen

as if intimate

invisible constraint

as if tempered

as if conditions prevailed.

NIGHT NEWS WITH FAKE ZEBRA

Let us move more quickly, night,
now night, star-encrusted, opulent.

The indictment of thought
is an opal's smooth version.

Guard our sensations, be copious
or at least perform adequate

vistas. I saw a pair of eagles
from the train. The train trains on.

They, their sitting.
Night: longer than their perch.

We: gathered and copious.
The eagles: a pair.

I warrant the arrest of the boy
who shot another boy in this sad.

In this sad, would you have said no?
Bickering, passing the gun, a game

of pass the gun.
There are gangs.

This is not a lesson.
A transformation of the subject

into another subject. Not to insist.
Velvet Revolution, Velvet Underground.

Lou, hello Lou? Can you hear?
I am here in the dark church

imagining an improvised history
as if channeling the news.

The eagles sit at the edge of the river.
The camera is out of earshot. Jack

Spicer is about to speak
into the nearest phenomenon

while the deer
while the dear

spelled d/e/a/r
halts naturalism

and a new equation
only you in the pews can solve.

Are we lost among our subjects?
The lone bobcat

Andrew and I saw
traverses

an ancient and incendiary
commotion. Hunting season

under the big tent.
And then there was a magician

strolling along in broad daylight
with something up his sleeve.

There is a silver zebra
on a silver tray in a gallery in New York.

to Michael Joo

AFTER NEWTOWN

Maybe there's a top at the end of
the world made by someone else.

Maybe it spins and becomes a blur
of river and sounds

windy. And the girl
who arrives and who gets to hold

the top at the end of the world
and to pull and push

so that it spins into blue rivers
seems never to die.

A train passes on the ridge.
The hemlock branches wave.

UGLY SONNET

Shame vanquishes the old school.
Truck stop rape. A or the women

falls or fall under the wheels
of chatter around truck stop rape.

Besieged by glare; the untidy
aperture of historical accounting for

truck stop rape. Flare of paper in wind.
Some sirens, some typing on small

handheld instruments. Minimal
delay but very little inclusion beyond

truck stop rape. Everywhere she saw
eyes looking back into the harbor

where there had been an accident and
no chance to escape the truck. Stop rape.

WORLD CUP

The world allows   stop me at any point

I am so sorry   *idea symbol procedure*

allows for   tennis   Roger Federer

try not to consume the view   I am really sorry

after the fact   after   more than a few

flying in the face of necessity   allows

for error   invariably corrected   the world

corrected   I am very sorry stop me at any point

down below captured   Roger Federer

the world allows you ask   what is this world

clarity   a procedural game   not   if then

not   consequential   openly

distributed   stop me at any point   motion

transparent   you can see a match   pass

to pass   Roger Federer   or hear

the noise of bees   oceans of bees.

to Nick Keys

MEANWHILE, STORM

All these   concrete   things
blown about

habitat of improvisation

heavily adorned

                        phenomena   do not grasp

motion
unmoored

under the catastrophe tent

limb rocked
pictures

had been
root-bound

                or truculent   not following not how

the brown lisp
tunneling up through spawn
shorn

and disobedient
as if duplicating

not the stiff buck
not journalism

pecking at our wares
and the beautiful illusion
also spawns

sea in cloud
basking on its throne

film trashed
in the forgotten

as the already
known

deception
in the black hall

the relinquished sequence
abundant with numbers

bitterly loaded

patched on to the original
sent out as flood.

IL PLEUT

And the ghosts of Galileo
and Apollinaire

are meeting in a room
reserved for those

in mourning for
acts of insight

that link
perception

to understanding.
They inhale clouds

that promise a more
thorough oblivion

than mere death.
There's a knock at the

horizon. Someone
has come to join them.

She is clothed in
white and,

like them, is
invisible to them.

She speaks slant
lines only the birds hear.

to Ron Padgett

A chair

and a painting

are in love

they resemble

each other

this happens

rarely

it takes a

long time

for a chair

and a painting

to fall in love.

One of them

is geometrical

and slides

across curves

against

a black ground.

The other

is floral.

The floral

once had a

fraternal

twin rug

but it was

exiled.

to Anselm Berrigan

UTENSIL

Track the quick-footed *more*.
Slack crib, fluid in another
mystery. Repeat after me.

There was a form after all
but not recollected.
Never look back. Do not sleep.

Skinny little day. Shadow
under the streetlamp.
Girl slender also, girl advent.

Repeat after me. Turn
slowly to look back
to where the footprints were.

Seek brevity. Don't look down.
There are some evolving stones.
The sky? There is no sky

only the task ahead.
Ahead, the easily erased.
Repeat after me. Count her

astonishing steps, feet
in snow, feet in clouds.
Do not look up.

Cold ricochets a blistered void.
We're in the ghost field now
driven across the drain bed

into the bowl of a spoon.
Things collect. Drops, etc.
blown into images, pink and red.

Don't look away. Do not sleep.
Repeat after me. Never let
her hand touch your mouth.

The long elation of our candor collapses in a small yard.
Backwoods, incessant beats. Backwoods, the very nerve of fidelity.
But say something else. Say the graphic doodles
our condition into froth in the arguing hills over there.
The days perish, wanting simplest ties.
And the flexible branch lifts and falls, a kind of wave.
Sooner or later we will enter Abraham's drum
and the wet slide of his hair
will abolish our simple roomlike conditions.
The invisible slope will drain into drops
while Abraham beats and beats his forgiving set.
Are the ancient songs contested? Are we too long
in the cave, on the island, in an insular, petty drift?
Questions are stained cups. The heart skips a beat.
Abraham wanders off in a mood of melancholy triumph.
The others, his mistresses, huddle on the floor.
His mistresses are part of the inventoried world:
they can be counted, they can be sent away
to join others, parts of others, they can be treated
like sentences in the inventoried world. See?
Their rush of silver and skin,
their elastic torsos bending,
their sonic reverb, gaping mouths.
Soon, they will become an incandescent spray
that Abraham will arrange in the harbor.
Do not shut the windows. The sounds from the sea
are important. They resemble notes, or drops.
Abraham resembles Abraham but is not Abraham.

to Abraham Gomez-Delgado

BASEMENT TAPE

Now comes

as a vanishing

so be it   a vanishing

not political the day was not political

although misery of exception although

there are those soon to be

disappeared

        massive injunction

           in the little dialogues with

   the held

all so

inconsequential among

a starved

      among a twilight.

The sexual apricot depresses me.

Come forward little migrant

orange emblem.

Come into the iterated

without a face, but, yet, with

a pit.

Glorious pit.

Glorious structure of inner abatement.

O give it up!

Give up the image!

Give up the announcement of the image!

Give up the spectacle!

Give up the announcement of the spectacle!

Give up the thing and its image and its spectacle!

As we were saying by the unlit fire one night, as we were saying.

And the swimmer—you know the one I mean—his torso!

Like a ship!

UNDER THE SIGN

Having dreamed of my dead sister
raging with urgent

need, she
conducting us through intolerable

passages, now forgotten, I
have burned my right hand

after sunset
small dark clouds above

the river I cannot see
while listening to

a scratched CD of a Haydn
piano sonata so that

certain passages
rapidly repeat

and having spent some moments
thinking of the vision

that accommodates
all that is unforeseen

as the world now
becomes without sequence.

It is impossible to say anything else, Alice said to herself. I think everything has been said, so the only thing to do is to repeat what has been said but to repeat it somewhere unexpected. I suppose this is what writers do, or some of them. It's a little like a baseball that starts in the pitcher's glove and travels to home plate and then gets hit far off into the stands, changing its history as it goes. I wonder if this is a good analogy, she said to herself, and then decided it wasn't at all, that she had confused the elements of the argument, so that saying or writing something had become a baseball. There was some kind of difficulty between the immateriality of thought and the materiality of a baseball, even one with Babe Ruth's signature on it, which could be worth a lot of money.

Money seemed to negotiate this place between the immaterial and the material.

The day was windy, the leaves were already partly down from their niches, bittersweet vines were crawling and twisting around the trunks. She walked down to the river, which gave off a strong, brackish odor that reminded her of the sea. Perhaps, she thought, if you do one thing every day at the same time you feel better about the way everything shifts around you, and you are not sure of your relation to these shifts—if you are part of them, or apart from them. What if you decide to be tossed from pillar to post, and not attempt to hold on? What does one hold on to anyway? What pillar and what post? I wish I could hold on to the light, but that is an impossibility, the same as holding on to time.

I suppose that memory is a way of holding on to time, but it seems to me quite inaccurate and clumsy, compared to a tree with its rings or a skeleton, both of which hold time much more firmly in place. I guess while we are alive there isn't any chance of holding on to anything. And then when we die, something or someone holds on to us, for a while, and then that goes away as well.

THE TEARS OF EROS

after Bataille

A format

thrown from purchase

exaggerated, a

wish-bloodied sign,

disoriented comfort, a

reversal played as habit

and fortuitous, a gaze

as if the image

could make its way

into desire's unmade bed

there configured by ghosts

and night's arrival

marked by force,

a vicissitude, pun,

or a chronic tryst

felt slowly between

lovers, bequeathed

and the essential veil

inward as soil

bitterly tossed

is thinly deceived

as mud and seed

not ever to capture

or recall but

to send again

the bliss quotient

also undetected a new

molecular dust

to open

now culpable

now nude now bare life

and emancipate

pictorial restraint

from veracity's cave

and the recalcitrant

disembodied

by silent advent

day's vigilant stare

flared into voice

and the bright air cries

for the street's permission

to liberate and revive

the conjurer's trick

among phantoms

blinded by fears his

enigmatic touch

drawn into wet tracks

another will attest so

the dissonant lament

lifts the prey

risks the broken

finds miraculous.

to Nathan Lee

II.

TASK: TO OPEN

TASK: TO OPEN

1.

I miss New York, a sense of living inside a rational plan—the grid—given over to spontaneity and complexity without measure. When I go there now I am sometimes overcome with a sense of abundance and familiarity; faces I pass seem to belong to persons I know, or once knew. The city seems to keep the past in play as active, uncanny material palimpsest. Passing the building on East Eleventh Street where I went to grade school. Footsteps. The dead.

Abundance of constant noticing, old practice of city life, before everyone looking at, speaking into, machines.

Now I live where flaws and ghosts are abundant, moving about in the winter air. Snow, and the heightened radiance of snow-clad branches: knowing that they are transitory, without meaning, without consequence. Why try to capture, in words, in pictures, to still or distill what vanishes even as it is being noticed?

Now it seems without point even as the word *spill* is close to tears: forgive this, I know we do not approve tears. The cat, dying, brings me to tears, a creaturely embarrassment similar to the augmented beauty of the snow-clad trees. Emily Dickinson:

> *We introduce ourselves*
>
> *to planets and*
>
> *to flowers*
>
> *But   with*
>
> *ourselves*

Have   Etiquettes

Embarrassments

And awes

2.

American mandate: be at once the *same as* and *different from*—
conundrum at the crux. Be all that, better than, more than! Be
normal, ordinary, unafflicted, unaffected by difference. My stu-
dents thrashing through these contradictions, trying to decide
what to keep and what to give up. To what does one belong? Po-
litical discourse stymied at the threshold of adamancy.

Language on this tightrope.

The idea of having something in common, the Commons; the
singular person and the crowded arena, village green, agora; Pla-
to's *Republic*; Times Square. Social media blurring these temporal-
spatial distinctions. We meet now in Nowhere.

The Strange approaches, ill-equipped to bring forward a
method to ease difference from the contagion of the same.

An obligation of art: to allow for these conditions to be fruitful,
contested.

3.

From Emerson's *journal* about his visit to Malta, February 1833:

*A few beautiful faces in the dancing crowd, & a beautiful face is always
worth going far to see. That which is finest in beauty is* moral.

Did Emerson pause between the first and second sentences? Did he note the beautiful faces in the crowd—not petals—and then get up and take a walk before adding, *"That which is finest in beauty is* moral*"*?

4.

Reading Roland Barthes's *The Neutral* causes awe at the apprehension of his inquiry; notational array, thought-sparks, marginalia, arising from what seems to be the functional generosity of doubt: doubt as engine of curiosity; the merging of skepticism with something akin to the structure of belief, but not in anything absolute or specific. So that belief is part of what it means to be affected by thought? the very terms of thought? *That we can know.*

Writing as the permeable edge between inward meditation and outward connectivity; in a sense *about that,* pulse and elastic flicker of the subject-object dyad that defines acts of being, reading, listening. These are acts of delicacy and attention, to allow for an opening, to let something unknown in, let it combine with what is already there. How else do we change? How else love?

5.

Many *ones.* Snow on ground accumulates. Shootings in Tucson; shootings in Newtown. How events invade without filter, without choice. The far is always already near.

Thinking that there are too many; one feels simultaneously remote and overwhelmed by a crowd inside solitary confinement. This sense may be both tendentious and obvious. Not interiority but welter of accessibility and exposure, the incessant streaming that makes the urban, by contrast, seem gentle, particular, slow.

On the computer, revisions are lost. To *save the changes* is to erase them.

Writing as temporal trace of a singular presence, different from film or photography; closer, perhaps, to music. Listening to music and reading enable a kind of time travel. At stake: the possibility of a particular form of reciprocity, intimacy. Something about actual touch; touch in relation to presence. How the virtual confounds this.

6.

The psyche jumps—old toy, doll or clown—brought into fantastic focus and then cast aside into the dump; internal drama played out against diffuse rituals. The question of intensities unmet by reality and so of excess. Shaky autonomy of being a self, capable at times of dividing into proximate agitated figures, provenance of fiction and dream.

Making a painting, a poem; making or being in love; reading: these *open* time from the prison of the clock.

Lisa Robertson, in "Time in the Codex":

The substitution of personae for self, of a series for an origin, of a rhythm for a state: Here is love's tension, love's politics. Here is form. The reader loves without knowing. I read for the book, simply because the book is there to be read. Sometimes my fidelity is for materiality.

I face something delicate and fragile that could span a great distance and then it closes. One time cancels the other, exercises its authority upon the other. I am suspended between form and perception, inflected with an outside temporality. Attention becomes impersonal.

7.

In our current climate, concept trumps percept: a requisite under-lying or anchoring idea seems to guide what we value in art and poetics.

Task: not to lift what *is* into what *is not*.

The imagination is the grace of *what could be*. Transcendence is the grace of *what is not*. I learn a new word: *apophasis*: unsaying, saying-away: the unsayable.

Plotinus to Celan to Beckett.

Wittgenstein: *"What we cannot speak about we must pass over in si-lence."*

8.

Empirical knowledge refutes mythos.

Wallace Stevens ("The American Sublime"):

But how does one feel?
One grows used to the weather,
The landscape and that;
And the sublime comes down
To the spirit itself,

The spirit and space,
The empty spirit
In vacant space.
What wine does one drink?
What bread does one eat?

Desolation of the real—landscape, weather—*empty* and *vacant* without symbol, ritual: Blood and Body. Stevens negotiates this obdurate deficit throughout; this is his bravery in the face of the ascendancy of rational empiricism; a consummate understanding of a perhaps infinite, restless permutation (the *possible*) that swerves beyond mere logic. Frank O'Hara ("Personism"): *"Pain always produces logic, which is very bad for you."*

The sound of wind and a constant nodding as if everything were in agreement with everything else, *yes yes yes*: the world is not a dichotomous monster being pursued by techno-giants with unspeakable skills, but instead is a dilation opening into fluid arrays, permissions, and potentials. This chorus seems insufficient in the face of technological negation, as we turn from the merely sensed, intuitive guide that, listening, awakens us to follow, to find.

From time to time we are *summoned* to transgress, or trespass, or just to be in an imagined *elsewhere*. The affirmation you are witnessing is blessed because it cannot know itself and therefore cannot find itself. Wind picking up, moon before long, hugely full, to rise. Poor overburdened Eros, asked to step into the breach between fact and feeling, into the very *fact of feeling* (William James).

9.

William James: the pragmatic method: *"the attitude of looking away from first things, principles, 'categories,' supposed necessities; and of looking towards last things, fruits, consequences, facts."* A kind of elasticity in relation to decisions, so that the past has no final jurisdiction over how the future might unfold; a tenuous relation to tradition as such; a form of curiosity that enables risk to occur without jeopardizing the discovery, or the perpetuation, of value. But we still need to ask: what value?

10.

Robert Rauschenberg's art a matter of putting things next to other things; next to, beside, around, above, under; primacy of the preposition throughout late modernity. Knowing only *as relation* (Rancière). In the service of an arrangement that is not lifting elsewhere, not transcendence. What he, Rauschenberg, inherited perhaps from Matisse, great master of *exaggerated* or distorted arrangement, but not Cubist, not collaged enjambment, not about either the flat plane or edge; ease and generosity in compositional relations, these as the actual form of perception in which we are invited to dwell. Rauschenberg's constant amusement, self-delight, games and finesse with words, origins, placement, displacement, borders, layers. Pleasure here distinctly neither guilty nor recondite.

A friend, an architect, remarks that he thinks the desire to arrange material objects in a room is a form of optimism. I recall the joy of installing a show in a gallery. This delight in arrangement is not bound by culture, taste, age, or class.

11.

Integrity must be the site in which intention and action are as one, in unison, seamless, without abrasion; *neurosis*, that idea we rarely hear of anymore, pulls us away from what we most intend and most want to do. There is a rip, a wound, and so we attempt to heal in the place where this wound recurs and cannot leave it be.

The poem forms around the impulse to find out what is going to happen to the poem. If one is under constant revision, does one lose integrity? Integrity (*whole*) as a form of the *same*. The *same* as an idea of consistency. But humans are flexible in being, in bearing; we shift demeanors in relation to others, an Other. As we change, we animate the historical pulse. Fashion pretends to reflect these shifts, but often is mere preening mask. Art is a better shape-shifter, both avatar and response to what informs. Charles Olson: *"what does not change / is the will to change."*

12.

Poet Charles Wright was featured on PBS. He talked about his late style as being more stripped down; he says his poems come from going out into his backyard and *waiting*. Poem as *stigmata*.

The work of art is already in the realm of the unreal; it attests to the way the unreal enters reality.

Habit, habitat, inhabit, habitual. The monk's habit; Saint Francis in his soiled robe. Etymologically connected to the Latin *habere*, to have and hold. The range of meaning distributed between *habit* dress and *habitude* custom. Also to temperament, disposition, and the native environment of particular species; also the lovely *habitué*.

Language *is* an astonishment; it never betrays its capacity for renovation. Why, then, do we rush to turn it to purely instrumental purposes?

13.

Andy Warhol was a radically lonely person, as far as I can tell, and he attracted to him other socially alienated persons, gathering them into his Factory. The notion that one might be released from normative relations—to church, to family, to community—guided his vision of a culture increasingly dominated by the persuasive tropes and signs of media and advertising. All this is now familiar. Warhol's relation to these topographies of mediated iconography was prescient in its anticipation of the banality and addictiveness of our culture's incessant *twitter.*

I think Warhol's vision was seeded in his Catholic upbringing; the martyrdom of Jesus that reaches its endgame in the transgressions of capitalism, where transcendent promise, a human idea, is perverted into markets indifferent to the specificities of individuals except insofar as they can be conscripted into their forces. Warhol's stated desire to be a machine was an ironic commentary on the way capitalism behaves toward persons; as if to say, in order to live, one must denude oneself of specific affective registers—joy, for example, or despair. *Machines do not feel.* In this fallen world, good and evil are playmates, and desire loses its specificity, its capacity to articulate difference. Choice mimics freedom. Warhol's painting of Marilyn, ensconced in tarnished gold, where the visage of a single person radiates into myriad evocations of a tragic historical momentum. What might he have made now when techno-spirit adumbrates the human as avatar of the human?

14.

Freeman Dyson, reviewing James Gleick's *The Information: A History, a Theory, a Flood*:

Information is independent of the meaning that it expresses, and of the language used to express it. Information is an abstract concept, which can be embodied equally well in human speech or in writing or in drumbeats. All that is needed to transfer information from one language to another is a coding system.

What, then, *is* the relation of information to knowledge? Is knowledge the way information becomes meaningful?

15.

Open: dilation greeted by a perceptual space that blurs outlines of things—*quiddity*: the what, the I—and releases them from their names, so that the stitch of linguistic attachment is broken or suspended; a temporal-spatial enlargement, eliding dualities; evacuating signified and signifier, forgoing the sign. An immense breath that is different from normal physical *in and out.*

Ann Hamilton's huge white curtain across the massive space of the Park Avenue Armory, "the event of a thread," its motion controlled by the action of swings, persons on swings.

In the face or fact of being in the event, limits of language: splendid abrasion. The beautiful word: *qualia.*

16.

A conversation the other night with Michael Brenson about Willem de Kooning, whether there was any way of perceiving what Michael calls "intimacy" through the paintings. We were thinking about the difference between de Kooning and David Smith, where Smith somehow allows us "in" to the complexity of his being; the sculptures embracing internal complexity and contradiction, managing to make them visually evident; we feel we are inside them, their discomfort, whereas with de Kooning, we can only gaze *at* them with a kind of awe. I felt, going through the recent retrospective, that he was *thinking through paint*, but that the thoughts were not to be opened up; a kind of shut, although luminous mask. The lush, sensuous gestures of the gesture, signs of embodiment, materiality, apprehension of the phenomenological weather of the world: all this oddly deictic.

17.

Events of a summer: oil spill: dry heat: need for morphological shift rather than mere hybridity: a slide through or across forms changing their *nature*: inventory of new shapes to include old shapes: the refrain: Deleuze and Guattari: *A Thousand Plateaus*:

A child in the dark, gripped with fear, comforts himself by singing under his breath. He walks and halts to his song. Lost, he takes shelter, or orients himself with his little song as best he can. The song is like a rough sketch of a calming and stabilizing, calm and stable, centre in the heart of chaos. Perhaps the child skips as he sings, hastens or slows his pace. But the song itself is already a skip: it jumps from chaos to the beginnings of order in chaos and is in danger of breaking apart at any moment. There is always sonority in Ariadne's thread. Or the song of Orpheus.

To ask what binds a community across a series of singularities: tacit care: this form of love is not familial, cannot be familial: the familial is always binding: obligation to love: brother says *I love you because you are my sister, but I don't like you.* To love within the context of an open set, so that within this set things might change, migrate, alter position, with a view to inclusion without possession.

The song, the refrain, the chorus. The hopes, desires, and values that underpin or inform community behaviors.

Asking for help via the Internet:

Does anyone have an X?
Can I catch a ride to Y?
I lost my Z. Has anyone found it?

Interchanges undirected to one person: can someone, anyone, help? Optimism. But optimism grounded in the possible, circumscribed by physical nearness: *site*. Notions of *place*, locale, incident, here, home, rootedness—all these begin to feel quaintly metaphorical.

18.

Task: *difficulty* as positive value: an arrangement that de-arranges: counterintuitive: examined life without the hindrance of chastising inner scold: birds covered in oil: unleashed event or episode without traction of adequate response so that consequence is adrift: spill: accident: nothing leads to anything: the paradigm.

Giorgio Agamben:

A paradigm is a form of knowledge that is neither inductive nor deductive but analogical. It moves from singularity to singularity.

Thinking of cells, invasions, mutations.

19.

Task: to confront this fact: to make something, say a work of art or a poem, that no one is waiting for, no one actively wants; without *market*: what comes into being, what arrives or materializes, is not expected, not announced: the unforeseen: not a child: moving into, becoming the place of the not yet desired: the poem as signature of that which appears without being invited or anticipated or wished for: untethered freedom: lassitude: why bother: for whom to write: *for myself and strangers* (Stein).

Constraint of formal, *invented* necessity: Harry Mathews: *twenty lines a day*; Oulipo; Jackson Mac Low: poem as production without the burden of subjective doubt or assertion: *appropriation*: take what is already there and recombine it: recycle without subjective/affective interference: mechanical angel: forfeit singularity without in turn creating community. Individualism displaced onto conceptual moves: Duchamp's genius.

The idea of the ordinary.

20.

Task: to ask what is the foundation of knowing: the unknown surrounds and defines: so *boundary* as instantiation of the known: knowledge as fluid, constant recombination and renovation (language): Deleuze's sense of the immanent: immanent life carrying with it the events or singularities that are merely actualized in subjects and objects: an almost mystical view, from Lucretius to modern physics.

My dream of death: luminous atomic particle-arc falling across and through the curve of eternal time-space.

21.

[A]n event horizon is a boundary in spacetime, most often an area surrounding a black hole, beyond which events cannot affect an outside observer. Light emitted from beyond the horizon can never reach the observer, and any object that approaches the horizon from the observer's side appears to slow down and never quite pass through the horizon, with its image becoming more and more redshifted as time elapses. The traveling object,

however, experiences no strange effects and does, in fact, pass through the horizon in a finite amount of proper time.

Crossing of boundaries: no origins, no states: roots: routes. Nomadic: fancy name for homelessness: move across, move through: be watery: the beautiful necessity: figure of Hermes. Figure of the stranger. Exile.

22.

John Ashbery ("The New Spirit"):

Because life is short
We must remember to keep asking it the same question
Until the repeated question and the same silence become answer
In words broken open and pressed to the mouth
And the last silence reveal the lining
Until at last this thing exist separately
At all levels of the landscape and in the sky
And in the people who timidly inhabit it
The locked name for which is open, to dust and to no thoughts
Even of dying, the fuzzy first thought that gets started in you
and then there's no stopping it.

Music/sound moving across, crosses boundaries: *the locked name for which is open.*

23.

This-ness overwhelms. Flood of response, a form of delirium, like an overexcited child. This is what happens: intensity of attention and attachment begins to dissolve into an excess of reception, apprehension that veers toward ecstasy. Language breaks open into pure existential assent.

A desire to collide: *look at, read, listen to this!* Not exactly, more like: *be in this with me.* So: unobtainable intimacy.

That we can know each other at all. Miraculous.

24.

A Thousand Plateaus. "1837: Of the Refrain" begins with a child in the dark, singing a song for comfort. Then home. Then:

Finally, one opens the circle a crack, opens it all the way, lets someone in, calls someone, or else goes out oneself, launches forth. One opens the circle not on the side where the old forces of chaos press against it but in another region, one created by the circle itself. As though the circle tended on its own to open onto a future, as a function of the working forces it shelters. This time, it is in order to join with the forces of the future, cosmic forces. One launches forth, hazards an improvisation. But to improvise is to join with the World, or meld with it. One ventures from home on the thread of a tune. Along sonorous, gestural, motor lines that mark the customary path of a child and graft themselves onto or begin to bud "lines of drift" with differ-ent loops, knots, speeds, movements, gestures, and sonorities.

Task: to reconfigure the Open into the normal, a pattern, an *ordi-nary*: so the extraordinary can be folded into the prior and the yet to come without breaking. Improvisation: to wander.

25.

Contemporary poetry, since late-century: a certain nudity, de-nuded, as if we were standing in front of a doctor. The return of the sentence. The disavowal of mystery. The empirical cool. Jour-nalism.

Counterexamples within this frame: tracks at the horizon of perception, as Mei-mei Berssenbrugge's long lines: the intimacy, the *extension*, of her concentration. Michael Palmer's relentless interrogation through the naming of what is along the edge of skeptical wonder. Younger generations indifferent to avant-garde yokes and doctrines, liberated and liberating.

These iterations of the *pragma*: William Carlos Williams allowing it into or onto *Paterson*; Charles Bernstein, in "recalculating," bringing the violent rupture of his daughter Emma's suicide into the fabric of the poem as if it were at the same level as everything else, so that its effect is one of an immeasurable undoing *from within*. Robert Creeley, famously, slight curb between written and spoken; this often the only way you could know or discern that the poem had begun as he reminisced about this and that: the minute shifts in cadence, pace, inflection; voice the insignia of poetic affect. Intensity spread out or distributed across or into the ordinary, a kind of diction, vernacular, *what can be spoken* I think Pound commanded (and did not follow); George Oppen's unflinching materialist gaze; so-called avant-garde postmodern resistance to subjectivities, aversion to intensity heaped onto lyricism heaped onto self; new poem as a form of, testament to, scholarship, "objectivity."

Register of affect as performance and in trajectories of subversive resistance, identities, genders, where actual uncomfortable, risky cultural shifts are found. Radical forms produced by historical necessity; not spurious avant-garde "moves."

Is *soul* found, *formed*, at the juncture of mind-heart? Marilynne Robinson (*When I Was a Child I Read Books*): "*Modern discourse is not really comfortable with the word 'soul,' and in my opinion the loss of the word has been disabling, not only to religion but to literature and political thought and to every humane pursuit.*"

Greek word for soul: *psyche*. Blame Freud's analytic for the loss of *soul*? Blame prerogatives of white secular liberalism?

26.

Day breaks into petulance: later, gestures become slights, insults. I read about hospice care and the dying *surrounded by family*, a sign of a life well lived, of fidelities and loyalties.

Rob Fitterman flies out to California for a day or so, to see our friend Stacy Doris in her last months. Thinking about someone is not the same as being with someone.

A friend dismayed at not getting to her mother's side in time; my own sorrow at not being near for my mother, for my sister, my aunt, my cousins, dying. Sister, moaning on the bed, in Washington; in New York, informed she is now dying, I am unable to act, to get up and go: turned to stone. *If I don't move will time stop?* A collision between what should happen against what is happening. The Closed.

To arrive the next, the following day into her already death; the train moving through or into her *not being alive*; the singular loneliness of grief as a measure of what the beloved will not now know.

When I asked Leslie Scalapino's husband, Tom White, about her being "ready" to die, he said she had no interest in it, was not resigned to it, thought "no poet should die," because they, we, have too much work to do! Onward!

Emily Dickinson's letter:

Ah! dainty—dainty Death! Ah! democratic Death! Grasping the proudest zinnia from my purple garden,—then deep to his bosom calling the serf's child!

Emerson asked: *Are they my poor?* I might ask: *Are they my dead?* Many ones.

War.

27.

The notion that, among creatures, humans have no natural capacity, are bare, and so were forced to make tools: "a matter of instruments." The instrument or tool: Mind itself, not something external to it. Is Mind language? Meanwhile, Mind continues to invent instruments to replace itself, speed itself, take over parts of itself: *our machines, ourselves.* In the *Times* an article on the end of forgetting: indelible traces or tracks on the Cloud that cannot be erased.

Task: garden.

 Temporal-spatial limbo

  sifting through the dawn

 awning drawn up

  embarking

  toward the opening in the circle

  this would be

 a ritual harmony of the singular

  tracing steps

   the pond beyond

 glossed

   sails the meticulous dress

as she departs

her circumstances.

Not to belittle the cause. We remain alert

despite oppressive

march

drone

on into another war in another climate

to—

the killing machine

embracing the desiring machine—

shadow   over

corpse.

28.

Irritant of lost time: immaterial repetition.

Setting down the track and then following, in the belief it will
come out somewhere; the coming out dependent on the setting
down. These narrative fictions constrain multiplicity

skips and gaps and snags, frictions and reroutings, repetitions
and   returns.

Thought experiment: imagine what a person might want to read in one hundred years.

Not about the new clarity of an evening light unless that light illumines something. Memory overvalued?

What troubadours?   Blasted outward

       toward the sink

     get in line   travesty of the incomplete

      toward utility

       its stench.

Sun on its way under but what? Horizon vanished.

The sea, the sea: that life itself is *buoyant,* will hold you up!

South African artist William Kentridge: protest as quickly shifting morphological abundance: lucidity, wit, and motion; intelligence as an inquiry that informs, or reveals, value.

This, then—form—how information finds its potential to mean. Has new technology been mistaken for form?

29.

I get up, make coffee, and begin to reread Baudelaire's *Paris Spleen.* Acuity of his rage, consciousness in relation to rage, perhaps the acuity of the fact of consciousness as the site of persistent rage—*spleen*: the City the site of a disjunction between the world as observed—things, persons, creatures—and the world as or in thought.

Something there: an unraveling of the seam/seem that stitched world to word. Is this in part what moved and animated Walter Benjamin?

30.

Get better at it! Scold, out of energy, ambition, music. It was not a good idea to look out. It was a worse idea to look inward, where just that morning an object not recognizable as among the living but nevertheless alive had removed another tooth from her mouth and performed some other unseemly acts before she had had my first cup of coffee. Where then? To the side, an open page sizzling with merit and glee. Under the desk, a lame match barely visible on the sand carpet. Up at the cornice where an intricate tracery of shadow hovered and writhed, depending on the speed of wind. If one could look at sound, if one could leave the door to the dream slightly ajar, if one could, for once, refuse another nut. But the thin, empty boat of shell, pristine as only a shell can be, not far from the single oatmeal grain, with a slit up its center, a whole continent away from the other, larger shell, the one from the sea, wretched with black ash whose stench bears no resemblance to that of the roiling waters from which it had come, a ruffled scallop, its wide mouth hinged to its twin, innards intact; the tiny shell was proof that the nut, the pistachio, had been consumed. In the unblistered snowy landscape she could almost hear the waves crash, see the waters recess while at the same time sinking, rendering the sand a thick paste where footprints had, only moments before, been perfectly visible. She could also hear, over her right shoulder, male voices and the occasional crack of the fire and the train reassembling the air into a loud rustle that seemed to merge with the wind.

Calamity has forsaken vocabulary and is going on ahead, without our utterance to keep it company. From the back, it looks innocent enough, certainly not dangerous, like a slightly hunched, slightly rotund cow that is beginning to sprout something that looks from a distance like purple thorns. Unique enough to cause the casual tourist to stop to snap or take or capture a picture; these days, the exact verb for this action is pretty much up for grabs. Something like snatch, or snag? Snag a picture. No, still too abrupt and noisy. It needs stealth. Swipe a picture, just like at the checkout counter.

Stop the car, Honey, I want to swipe a picture of that cow!

Anyway, the cow is lumbering on just at the edge of the tide and seems to be heading for the dunes, and then on into the mountains. Hard to say what, if anything, she is after.

At some point it will be dark just as at some point the cow will return. This is one of the facts that doesn't have to come with a money-back promise. That is why, she told me, she had to return the engagement ring. We were in a taxi after the recordings warning you to buckle your seat belt had been curtailed, heading uptown to an opening of a show by that guy, you know, the one who seals himself in an enormous Coke bottle filled with Coke and then tries to drink his way out of it? Just as we were headed into the curving tunnel over Grand Central, she explained about the ring. The one I had, an emerald, simply slipped down the drain.

31.

The dark is not an allusion to anything untoward. That primordial analogy has the characteristics of an absolute. Light: *good*. Dark: *evil*. But when you think about it, the reverse is often the case. I suppose, before electricity, the dark might have been construed as ominous. Even now, with the storm approaching, we make sure to have candles and such on hand, just in case. Just in case the flat, barren vista opens before you as you turn to kiss him on the mouth and feel the slight tug stirring below on a cloudy night without a single star to help you find your way home to the mercantile ravishment of new linens. Ah, Joni Mitchell: *"I miss my clean white linen and my fancy French cologne."*

The emerald was cracked. It had had another life before it came to me, and who knows, maybe others before that, time without end. Surrounded by small diamonds, it sat up in a high, ornate gold setting, its cracked green eye staring out, the diamonds wincing. Others have probably noted the word *gag* sitting inside of *engagement*. The original artifact was made of cloth, and large enough to place across the mouth of the beloved. The smile gag, it was called, a soft crescent scarf tied at the back, its tissue tails falling provocatively under her long tresses. Sometime toward the end of the century before last androgynous energies were unleashed, especially in the West, and so the smile gag found itself used by thieves to cover their faces during criminal acts; sported by cowboys around their necks at hoedowns. In the 1950s, teen girls once again took them up as "neckerchiefs." Or, *comme il faut*, "neckies."

She plucked the fine hairs under the chin. Her sufferance of fools did not exist, and under the heading "fool" she included all forms of destitution. She turned her back on the immigrant woman who wanted, in the midst of another opening for another show, to unburden herself of her trials on her journey from Kraków to America, losing everything in its wake. She ignored the fellow always seated under the canopy of the Korean deli's assorted flora, who addressed her with a dull familiarity: *How're you doin' today?* She kept her eyes forward, uptown. She stored these human impositions for a later moment when they emerged from her beautiful mouth as cunning, comic bile.

32.

The spark we do not see when we put the key into the ignition. Or when we turn up the heat, and the floor trembles as the furnace is called upon to heat the room. Life heat. Death cold. What to do? Another hot war, heat the planet up with fire, burn everything, the temples of course, and the fences—so what if they once made good neighbors? The hell with that; we need fire to heat our freedoms to boiling point, and then make some nice green tea. I like mine with honey and soy milk. The ice caps melting is outside of our current policy. It confuses the issue.

Coetzee:

"Pain is truth; all else is subject to doubt."
"I believe in peace, perhaps even peace at any price."

33.

The sky is good company. It refuses to accumulate, which makes it always first; the sky and music. These should be the elected guides for the new world order. The sky cannot repeat: most precious, most desirable. This particular light, that cloud, these colors, have they ever been before? I conclude they have not, although there is virtually no way to know; no proof. *Swipe, swipe.*

Emerson called his journals *Savings Bank*, *Blotting Book*, and *Wide World*.

February 1820:

These pages are intended at their commencement to contain a record of new thoughts (when they occur); for a receptacle of all the old ideas that partial but peculiar peepings at antiquity can furnish or furbish; for tablet to save the wear and tear of weak Memory, and, in short, for all the various purposes and utility, real or imaginary, which are usually comprehended under that comprehensive title Common Place book.

In another entry, from March of the same year, he imagines himself in a library, "costly, splendid and magnificent," where he

would "let my soul sail away delighted into . . . wildest phantasies."
Emerson is interested in the possibility of furthering motions of
the mind: "imaginations of enchantment." He hunts around for
figures whose writing can help him find how to inscribe thought;
he assesses the early journal: "It has prevented the *ennui* of many
an idle moment and has perhaps enriched my stock of language
for future exertions."

As if there were in fact *a first place* always in wait, like the sky.
This desire for an initial encounter; it spins out of the actual
reality—this stuff, these years—like a moth from its cocoon.
As if one could shed everything: a sense of panic and excite-
ment, anticipatory, exactly against the stasis of calm and yet
anchored by recessed attachment. *Trust* as always the crucial
element.

There are patches of blue; the clouds are thick and white with
dark gray underbellies; the river, a dull pewter. The inadequacy is
obvious: "blue," etc.

34.

Barges are plying the Hudson.

I don't like looking up and out and ferreting for the possible occa-
sion of the poem. O poem, where are you? Years ago I wrote a
poem called "East River Barge," written after a taxi ride up the
East River Drive, but the Hudson does not want to offer a sequel,
maybe because I am *static* as it moves. Poems as iterations of inter-
active motion.

What we retrieve hallucinates uneasily into morning.

Julian Barnes, in *The Sense of an Ending*, barely mentions the
weather, or anything phenomenological; the book is scant on vi-
sual description, nearly void of sensuous detail. The protagonist

doesn't seem to register these elements. This makes the writing both clear and arid.

35.

Last night looking out the south windows into the darkness, a huge light in the sky; *Star?* I wondered. *Star?* Huge and bright. At its side, the familiar three stars of Orion's scabbard. But the big light moved, it came closer, it had tiny red sidelights, it passed over, humming to itself. Am thinking this morning about restoration, about how the Occupy Wall Street became a holding place, marking the disquiet and unhappiness brooding across the country, the countries. You see it mentioned often in stories that are not about it; it points, the name seems so far to escape the ideological impasse that has immobilized the political landscape.

Malfeasance, indifference, cruelty, hidden under the tarp of self-interest and greed.

Awake in the night, trying to formulate something about Gertrude Stein's relation to description, wanting to come up with a phrase for what she does with the physical, material, visual world; her resistance to normative forms or linguistic structure which has fascinated into the postmodern poetic imagination. There is a way in which she proposes a *radical interiority*. (You see this in Picasso's portrait of her: the static monumentality, the obsidian eyes.) She seems to have experienced the world and all its objects as a vast interior structure that her writings somehow externalized: *exact resemblance to exact resemblance*, but not mimesis. Something about her dissolution of syntactical relation, subject-predicate, that haunts us. The myth of the pure *materiality of language*.

36.

Emerson, age seventeen, 25 October 1820:

*I find myself often idle, vagrant, stupid and hollow. This is somewhat ap-
palling and, if I do not discipline myself with diligent care, I shall suffer
severely from remorse and the sense of inferiority hereafter. All around me
are industrious and will be great, I am indolent and shall be insignificant.
Avert it, heaven! avert it, virtue! I need excitement.*

Wind sound: as if the dark were in motion, an inky processional
bloom.

Is there any way to measure or articulate the difference between
writing or reading on or from a page and writing or reading a
screen? What is the nature of this difference; does it matter? The
question will soon be moot. Ah, books, *the handwriting is on the wall.*

37.

Milky morning light. Squirrel headed up the maple with a mouth-
ful of leaves. Nesting. River gentian blue. Squirrel back down for
more leaves. Deep hole in the tree.

The word *estranged* hangs in the air; remnant bit of conversation.
The eyes stay a few seconds longer than they ought, or might. The
twilight god is up to no good. The core spot is activated as a form
of transport; the chip that harbors all the reticent energy awaiting
release. Phantasm arc, zipper across the world; *open* it. Let mind
embrace matter, let language subside into shared assent.

David Graeber (*Possibilities*):

*In the world posited by Medieval psychology, desires really could be satisfied
for the very reason that they were really directed at phantasms: imagination*

was the zone in which subject and object, lover and beloved, really could genuinely meet and partake of one another.

38.

Old question: is there such a thing as *disinterested* love? Love without either the desire to possess or the expedience of use: ultimate good inscribed in religious texts and figured in the democratic civic ideal: to choose the many over the one. In our new world order, this choice seems difficult to access, remote, blocked by stunted ideologies, a staging of self-interest that stymies the possibility of responsive thought attached to deeds *on behalf of,* for, the greater good; so much myopic friction, belligerence, animosity. Pious rhetoric of shared interest, sacrifice.

If I love a painting by, say, Philip Guston or Joe Brainard or Amy Sillman, is that love animated in part by a desire to own it? But then I want to say—with John Dewey—that an experience *is* a form of possession, something one *has.* I experience love for something or someone, and that love is what I possess; not the object of it. This is the side of Pragmatism often overshadowed by an emphasis on practicality and cool legal utility, outcomes or consequences uninformed by affects. The rational is pernicious if stripped of affect; reason *includes* it.

The experience of art shows us how to attach feeling to critical thinking, and so might inform, temper, how we act toward each other. Without this experience, we are set adrift in received, rigid ideas of the good. Art marks, demonstrates, the passage from the good to the just through the agency of care. To make something is to care for it. The *burden* of care. Etymology finds *grief, anxiety.*

The need to consider, to teach, human efforts and practices that do not immediately convert into practical utility or commerce.

Can the Internet be said to give us an experience, in this sense of fully *undergoing* something? There's something at stake here I cannot quite name, having to do with the relation of mental activities to material or physical presence: the embodied, the performed, the real or actual near. Anxiety that our sense of each other will be denuded of the spontaneous ensemble of minute readings—facial expressions, hand gestures, vocal inflection, smells—which until now have informed how we distinguish, for example, those we come to love or admire from those we fear or detest.

This is almost too basic but touches on an elision, a potential devaluating, of our creaturely beings.

Noema, when we doe signify some thing so privily that the hearers must be fayne to seeke out the meaning by long consideration.

39.

Surplus ubiquity of imposed critique and rampant opinion; nothing can be near under these forms of distantiation; embarrassed at the very site of our attachment to work: productivity, satisfaction, use, beauty, the Other. So *affect* as a kind of virtual nomad, wandering in the desert of permanent techno-reification.

"Underneath all reason lies delirium, and drift." (Deleuze)

40.

In any case the ghosts are awake, and fearful. They seem to believe that they are about to disappear forever from our thoughts like mere clouds passing on the horizon, skipping autumn leaves. Although they are now distinct from each other, they fear they will soon be only a remnant archaic category, itself replaced by a new generation that wafts around like so much decomposing smoke, detached from even the memory of the fire from which it rose. It will require a new name. This is what I am thinking while simultaneously aware of the fact that I do not believe in ghosts, nor do I know what the difference is between a ghost and a soul: two wayward nouns without objects. The new, renovated ghosts will be soulless and indistinct, mere zeros and ones for whom neither the peace of heaven nor the torture of hell makes any difference. These improved ghosts will have come from the old species as it set out to refine itself in the new age. Refine, and so be equipped to forget the treacherous complexities that made life before death nothing if not a vibrant passage of quixotic, mostly irresolute questions. The species will have tinkered among the twisted strands of the genome, pulling out unwanted threads, as it were, and replacing them with others, so that what was once a tapestry of variegated colors and textures will be as smooth and monochromatic as a pool of melted ice. The new nameless ghosts will float upon this pool.

41.

There was a leak in the kitchen ceiling from which water dripped into a red pail from time to time, making a slight splashing sound, rounded at the edges, so you could almost hear the indentation in the surface of the water as the drops fell. Some of the drops did not fall into the red pail at all, but fell instead onto the newspaper I placed on the counter under a second hole in the tin roof of the ceiling. The sound of this second leak, more infrequent than the first, was muted and flat.

III.

DEAR INSTRUCTOR

UNTITLED (SPOON)

Dear instructor, how to

clarify this momentum from its

singularity among thieves.

The tide was pink this evening.

I saw three deer, a rabbit, and a fox.

A visitor came, we spoke, he

gave me

amazing tomatoes

grown by the sun.

These mild occurences

and others insinuate

the forgotten as the retrieved and

the impossibility of any recovery

as such. I know, you are lost.

I am lost as well. We need

a table. We need

objects on the table. Say a spoon.

to Peter Sweeny

OF SPIRITS

Dear instructor:

Pound said

There is no provision

for them

and made none.

Seek below

the inscrutable flood

a node broken from care.

Not the sensuous

not the damn dream gouged

not the backward angel.

Not yet ice.

Rake up air

discern the altered start

tether it

word by word

to go on or beyond

reluctance.

Attach reception.

Animate.

LETTER (IN PRAISE OF PROMISCUITY)

Dear instructor,

no one is faithful. This is not auto-

biography. There's a clumsy note

on your doorstep

beyond orange bags at the roadside and

and this

apology for wanting to

to have spoken to you sooner.

We're sutured now.

A calm of sorts has taken hold and

and yet

technology is fevered.

Thought wishes everything were

were everything French

as in the living dead of the sad least genre.

The poem greets its bouquet.

I am thinking of floral wreaths.

They seem to have a story.

The story is not heartland pure.

The story yields a structure and

and the structure seems infinite.

The floral occasion is a circle.

This would be a trope for

everlasting or undead love

but the boy is gone. He stepped out over

over a crest of ocean into our own

perdition while we slept. In sleep, the lover

comes back. At first the lover is

is a cruel and indecipherable metonymy.

Then, or after, he seems

seems released from the triangular hood

hood worn as protection against infidelity.

Try not to think about numbers.

Numbers are a form of punishment.

UNTITLED (AGAINST PERFECTION)

All that left aside   left awkwardly on that side done away with

in immediate neighborhoods of chivalry. Wait. Under the

cleft sign to read will be continuance, a kept event because there was a

delivery of sorts. Because it had come to pass near?

Wait. Old ting-a-ling sat down sweaty

thought the portrait was of Mick, thought she had long hair

then, then stopped. Wait. And wanted these not to die

not to pass on. Wait.

The lad's charm charmed by the lad   his demeanor *thank you* so young

among the crowded   the high bed lifted charmed

while the gaze   without therapy   without the car.

Wait. She has this she has the left hand a paper

she has the kiss long afterward they had passed

had kissed in the smallest room had found the ring of fear

                   and still things happened, kept happening, went on

although the mode shifted in degree and measure. Wait.

Had these come withered now under such guise as the planet's remembered

cycles, their friction carried out against clouds, anxieties, waste, then what

was planted or planned would approach through the center of conviction—

yay or *nay*—butressed into abstraction, possibly scented with lemony

highlights in our visual age. Okay, I too have had it, the tale, the tremors, the

incidents so enjambed that only the edgy molecule catches on, breathes its

miniscule agenda onto skin like that of a peel.

The peel of evening across high bricks.

The peel of an orchid's deadly grip on perfection.

ZERO & A

1.

Usually biographical spill   never mind or con-

                   like a snowball in hell

         strain

against operations

of the sour physician

    her lesions or lessons, her

    blank-rimmed scan

    across the universal cup

—smashed dialectic of the entire.

2.

Usually biographical spill   never mind the oil

having opened the signature of all things

and peered into method

seeing there

that

a paradigm is only an example

repeated

        and the empire of the rule

hovering over the example

like a snowball in hell

smashed dialectic of the entire

the laws of form

        whereof Paracelsus speaks

        our alphabet

            strewn across

the *herbs, seeds, stones, and roots*

or then

    that

merciless recurrence of our nakedness

unmarked until remarked.

3.

The irrational disorder   usually

biographical spill

                    unintelligible quotient of the real

abstracted through love

and such invitations taken to mean

the con-

                sequences

                sequential

            humilities of virtue

revealed while awaiting execution

in the eyes of the law:

                        trick.

4.

Winged creature stranded in oiled starlight.

A shadow's weight filmed

without sound

unfurls toward its catastrophic bloom,

orifice of the ancient cave

                    concealed secrets deposited

borne flashing

into an astonished fount:

toxic flames pillage the air.

5.

Usually biographical spill   never mind

cold arcade

It is not that what is past

casts its light on what is present, or

what is present its light on what is past; rather,

image is that wherein what has been

comes together in a flash

with the now

to form a

constellation.

Look!

Deft market beckons toward a shelter, icon by icon.

Trespassing

the dying creature staggers across the path of

art's path

dragging omniscient sorrow.

6.

Zero is in love with A.

These accidents happen; they are signs of
things

to come. Ask anyone

ask the ghost

in the machine that speaks the code's

new emblems—

ask the crippled incubus

limping up the hill

ask the last of the evolutionists.

The child of Zero and A

is unable to

point at the thing that is

outside itself

       say that   star

        moves in swarms

          over the shadowless desert

         attaches

            to the arc

              waves

              under and over

and the radar of sound

       not *spirit*

       not spirit

we are embarrassed by spirit, the grid attests to this

          geometrical *spit*

     informing the cluster of being

       digital mime digital mime digital mime mime.

7.

Cast the small occasions of research

into a cup of

steady words—

forgive me

I am jumping with

instinct—

cast the apparition of time

into the play of integers

and their daughter N-7

forgive me I am

jumping with the unspent

as if it were a pardon.

A PLAN

Perhaps we should put all circles together

and then all squares. And let's

sequester blue from its neighbor

then ask it to perform in the biggest atrium.

In the greatest episode of an ordinary life

there is tenderness

but this is not recalled on an ordinary day.

The sequence, on an ordinary day, is mute.

It steals and flaunts, it has the animating

iteration of an impostor. Perhaps

we should put everything in a shelter.

The lament is recursive: *Jerusalem, Jerusalem.*

UNTITLED (FATE)

1.

Rescind the error margin   gap

adumbrated by the machine

mentioned with colored dots

during the wish for a separation

between sensation and trace

when we came close

        a kiss

     to suggest

       the indelible

    to be free from

       linguistic

          song of the thrush

    to move

       into the ungathered.

2.

The diction of the road

fails its intention.

We're on some other path

along sight lines

unpermitted to land.

Dear instructor,

is fate shaped by an idea

withheld from daily force

and from the thing I

thought I saw

on the grave of the unknown?

The iris is the color of a bruise.

The world is uneven in its orbit.

3.

Having not read the signs,

having missed the cues—

Absence.

A bowl.

Glassy.

A FOLD IN TIME

Not to swerve off the road
dust runs in the family

of the dream
speaking into the sheet

shrouded in you
in which you

shortly after the curtains
addressed the flood

the ratio
were detained, saying

repeated frequently
need to want spoken

near the foxed copy of Yeats
under the stained eaves

had been abused
thematically after the earrings

whispered at the door
want to need ushered in

as the dream is not in the real
the door is not in the dream

rose cloth shade
hidden dark assembly

charged objects in space
what is called optimism

among the not dead
certain distributions

leaning toward the mouth
spoken in the

western sky
embrace or image

not biography although
this too, dear instructor,

and the thump of footsteps
that cruel intimacy

at the threshold
above the abrasion:

Did you cry?
Prayer spoken, arrested.

to Nat Tripp

1.

Gray wool rags

             peripheral rider

     a column has broken

      strained

        desert well

you haven't seen

        a girl's head against a white tent

   not blue

     not blue.

          Look where?

Some small

differences in shade

      form to form

a splinter on the road

the bait raining.

2.

Desperate empirical!

You see nothing   the drab *is* walks by

into the forgotten

into the shuffle

sun flaps its white wing

inhales the landscape

nobody is looking   nobody sees

sun

exhales poem.

UNTITLED (THE DISINHERITED)

1.

The writer's swan passes, quoted

in a dark interior.

As and *of* difficult.

No signal.

The photos, however,

are sincere. The light

dull on the swan

equipped with mean beauty.

Some motion

among those who belong

and those who visit.

Make no mistake.

The land, its uses, its

little shingles,

theirs.

2.

Among us we hunt the fickle root.

Slide on over, Hon.

My brim is too wide, I cannot

see out.

Earnest collaboration among birds.

Sing sweetly now that the branch is clean.

Fix the roof.

I'm warming up for the real thing

although I still can't hear you

under this sign, this

sky booth.

3.

Unblessed forum counters relative merit.

Truth vortex!

The day wet, late, wet, late.

The light, dull.

The barn massively pictorial.

The house massively perfect.

Barn not empty.

Barn full of the weights of the dead.

Here, have this, a clay

sculpture of a

naked girl

on her hands and knees

before a black thing.

                    .

4.

Gist trouble markets war talk.

The irreducible bad guys at the door.

The sad gray cadets.

Stone the infidel!

Vocabulary of lost causes

meets vocabulary of

found causes

and we and they

launch combat.

No signal.

5.

Of course the present

is open is

calamity in waiting is

marked

previously unharmed

in a frame.

The present is endangered.

Sell it.

6.

Incised on the heels of the domain

no time to set the sleeve   ratty logic

of the shield   misgivings

traced along the shore's bony apparatus.

Come back! A call in the septic dream.

The trees are marked for departure.

The river is laced with icy aisles.

7.

The negative is a posse! See how it rides

across the game, how it

spells exception after the ship, the ripped sail,

the extinguished horn, the engulfed mast

passed on. The one we love is

in this dungeon of blur, this mobile thread.

How lucid this is

depends on where you are from.

                Back home, shuffling

men in slippers, a woman asleep in a slip.

Or else, back home, she is

awake and the sun lays stripes on her face

through the blinds. We hear, more recently,

that the estate has been

abandoned, the marriage collapsed.

BEAUTY AND CONSOLATION (RICHARD RORTY)

Sometimes there's an altar:

        world, dressed

    flagrant & discerning

       stopped above   or   lines of flight

       arrested   seemingly arrested

an altar:

   quotidian in pace   a cart's wheel, a tag

        made for the mildest enterprise

to follow   and so   anticipate an edge

as if wanting to sail

or to move closer   along the periphery

    a table or cloth   or now a hole

    through which a needle

cannot pass

the sign having landed on the wall

in its garb of light

                        waiting for its name

after nature

            not web not wing   marked

for some better foil

than the diction of the real

            hovering   or   suspended   a call

                        to pivot on the unconsoled   as

an image

            drawn from the lover's pocket

                        into the nearly opaque blank

straining the ordinary from its only   or also   there

                        crawl space of the lungs   mold dust

not, dear instructor, auto-

biography

while listening to

Richard Rorty   talk of

          Nabokov

and

                    kestrel, cedar waxwing, rare

orchids, his hurt companion stymied.

to Joan Richardson

UNTITLED (THE RIVER)

1.

And Diogenes placed a crown of pines

on his head   victorious Diogenes

spitting in the face

of the ignorant teams

      Diogenes crowns the horse

who stood his ground

Diogenes

   the dog   illumined.

Because he said so

    trussed under the moon

the blessing garbled as usual

      forgiveness

spilled on all the stones.

Historical stones, as they were what

touched the core

trussed behind a shut door

under an invisible moon.

Because no one mentions

rust across the river

sun tissue   streaked or hairy

the familiar beasty hills

the atomic flaw

breasted and phallic

across the wide gray surface.

All this, dear instructor,

our material journey

blown onto a radiant scarf

as some remnant rhymed with

scant flow

or distilled into thought's

crowded integers   not to turn away

to acknowledge the tracks of sky

marking our way

            or drawn above

in such yields no market could furnish.

The affinities   their stake

at the terminal hour

        you will not recall the willow

        you will lie down

how on the train

others exist

along the way   passages

        her floral scansion

ripped

            the horizon divided

intelligence

of love's song to the ghosts

they or   Diogenes

                    who might

                prevail

reading   ashes   leaves   cards

no preference

among their habits   the ghosts

            bored at rush hour

                    among the gossips

knocking sparks from each other

the tide withstanding

habit   bored by any occasion

rising from lamps along the tracks

moving under a huge blue tarp

as if something had erupted

opening the book.

2.

But if love of data refutes mystery

must the philosopher walk away?

The poet is a procrastinator

and a revisionist. She observes

the river is for the birds. She recalls

the sacred Nantucket coast.

Her vision is empirical

even as a love of mystery refutes data.

Geese on the baseball field.

A flag, red tile, a metallic balloon.

The aggression of sorrow.

Marianne's orange jumpsuit.

Had better launch another trial

without jury

without the old cavern

endowed with a seamless, impervious argot.

If the last revolution

discovered silence

while the rest heard

    over the swerve

        a telltale scream

braided or sewn down onto the field—

    what now?

UNTITLED (THE NEUTRAL)

1.

That we might find here

that we might hope to find

expertise

descending

    or sleeping with everyone

        or guided by questions

the neutral

sitting like a duck on the river

as an argument

unbound in the face of it

the fact of it

and such easy equations

reminiscent scores

to trip out over the exquisite form

the ancient in rags

the past as an arrangement

        with knowledge

forgive these slight durations

the moments of prosody

outside our chamber

             haunted by an

articulate sublime

without coastal reference

without the bloodied narcolepsy of desire.

Try the pathos of ghosts on your side

the riven energies of need

        the rabbit is waiting

the sparrow is waiting

a creature lurks below the broken adage

and so beware of whatever is next

whatever has been left out

about to turn up

in the known stories of the home

—she ran away, he did not stay—

in the sarcastic iterations of the norm.

2.

Or instead we might find

the neutral

on a bright morning in

late July, and wonder, in this shade, what

is happening all along

the scintillant edges of time.

If *to mourn is*

to be alive

and if the shape of knowing

is only the shape of not knowing

what else is riding

along this edge

as it leaks

onto the shapes of things—

blurry cascade

unattached

until it touches

the evident.

Is that *this*?

Circling over the tidy episode

a constant

as of a bird over prey

the heart's insistent refrain

wingless as a chant

but then elsewhere

wandering

how the mind wanders

into the verbal shade

leaving and returning

iterated as echo or prayer

summoning from the shade

inarticulate benevolence

care enters the dismissal of care

drawn across the virtues of a stage.

3.

A rustling in the wings.

Restless mercurial

annoyance: nothing gets started.

You are waiting for me

but I do not appear, even in disguise.

The stage keeps unfolding its infinite domain.

At the final curtain, certain names

are cut into morphemes: *no* and *win*

fall from their origins in the adored dark.

Meanwhile atrocities are creased

into the percale

one by one, as if drones

left behind in a prohibited archive.

No one is writing this act.

Author! Author! calls the diminished crowd

wandering from the plummy sunset

caressing the hills. Backlit

hawks turn and turn above the scenery.

TO THE GIVEN

Dear instructor,
tonight I am

word poor and so   unchained
and the world seated

could be
sensed partially

your back to it my looking away
trace of a cry in the air

accumulating from afar
a clarity of means

because
entrenched in beloved

semblance

to climb into the given as

music or the simplest conduct—

touching the threshold

migrating

serene as matter or

untouched

traveling—the wind—

made only for space

perceived

as elegy's long flight.

And so

darkening chanced over the neck

the shoulder's ache

       not referral to the outside

  having not yet aspired

darkening yet

the test or turn savored

the instance   leaning forward

to hear

a song of some duration

shelter of what is not said

chanced, here and there, over, darkening—

      splendid matter erased.

Could look through to the voice—

could look to find where the voice—

have you a word,

dear instructor, for this?

City of words

rotunda and desert wanderer

    climb the absence

       follow this simple curve into the footprint

           or find indifference   a shelter

   as if lost within a cave

     confounded

        within the merry leafy compost

city of words

    ideal translation and misfortune

        to hesitate at the sequel to traipse backward onto the

path

     stunted underfoot to wait until the sugar dissolves

        until the rat's nose upends a leaf

          seeing as the windows are shut

       the heads are mounted on rose hips and thorns

        prayer is spoken into the dark

city of words

bring the ruin to its proper place among nouns

open its mouth   peer into the rosy throat

surely not a new day

her name is common

she walks along the fibrous tissues and sticks

recalls the fictive cause to save to go back   to align

to dwell among first attributes of space

but what are these?

Hasty dim angels.

Are they above, below?

Beautiful plural sloping toward duration.

SOME ELEMENTS OF THE POEM

1.

Restive valley/lucidity non-Olympic
squalor of the mundane

ushered, foiled, never golden/blessings un-
told/missed under the standing muscular artifact

she invoked/did not remain the studio scold
lover in negative shield

fled volition's study if to lie down if to hear
eyes assaulted so to sting

mouth on top of mouth in the hinged vernacular
thought's respite or *figura*

arrested in flight. Tact and the cradle jammed
an indecipherable setting across ligatures

of care. Patience and the cloth elbow of a monk
scribe to the half-life of angels/quick

fluidity of names/incantation waits for veracity
if to be sure is to be otherwise among stones

everything undone/inertial tread along
a patriotic map of stars. Voice into hole.

Voice stares not into anything seen but lifts
harmonic for glue in the dark

hot chapel under the patterned glass
and came here with a root in mind.

2.

Came flustered with concision, mother's
child face in copied blue her

skeptical smile out of hearing out
of hearing in view or Stacy's

inner ear stares into Lucretius:
atoms for Venus, roses for the lascivious

Miss Stein. Mother at the side of the
carriage/sister Alice

within earshot, smiling infant, smiling
love of the one smiling

back and Will said something about love
and I eyed his mouth and he said *diffuse*

what's the use? Mother
may have asked the question within

earshot like that dog. I like the middle voice.
The gesture could be simple

not exhausted not vestigial not a painter's
despair in the purple cowl of the monk's robe

in the elegant gallery shoes leaving shortly
for vacation in a small town in France

to read Edward Said writing on Genet
missing voice among many these voices

what is possible/to be
belated among the last ditch

of experience as sound among thieves
restless articulations of this time.

"Noises from the depths," Deleuze remarks,
"become voices when they find in certain

perforated surfaces (the mouth) the
conditions of their articulation."

3.

I like the cast of the crisscrossed fence pattern
on the driveway. Shadows belong to footage.

Everything belongs to something else.
The gesture/although I wish I were walking uphill

is to open the hand. I repeat: *open your hand.*
This to indicate, to sign, suggest

you are willing to give up holding on
or keeping or really in any way

imagining that you possess
anything. There's light on the wires.

The green is heavily green. August adds
weight to green. Walking uphill

with a friend I said
opening the hand, in response

asking the degree to which
to interfere with or keep kempt

nature in relation to the path
we were following, the surrounding field.

Ann Hamilton and I made a video
when I was in Columbus, Ohio,

visiting/a video of my hand
enacting or rather accompanying

a reading taken from Emerson's essay
"Circles," in which, it seemed to me,

O is a frequently repeated
soundscape. I don't think

but then I don't know
if Emerson thought about these

recursive *O*s, but
I felt or feel sure that

writers, some writers, respond
to different registers

of sense possibility. Perhaps this
observation goes without saying

but having said it
I will let it stand not exactly as

a statue or statute, but as a bringing
forth into the space of hearing

obvious or given acknowledgment
that sound conjures itself into

or while seeing what you say.
Here reminded of Lisa Robertson's

essay, in her book *Nilling*,
called "Lastingness," in which she

cites Jean Starobinski's citing Saussure's
idea of a "phonic matrix" in classical Latin

poems, finding "mannekins," isolated
"theme-words whose uttered sounds were

hidden, and sometimes scrambled, beneath
the overt textual semantics—a material substrata

of encoded sound." I don't think finding
repeated O sounds in Emerson's "Circles"

qualifies but it might be a vestigial
trace of this complex arena of sound sense

which I think in the new technological
dispensation is falling away from our shared

calling. "Let's listen to music," one girl says
to another, in affectlessness. Vacuity

or vestige of the gesture
caught between Venus and Hercules,

promise of the black elision, so to assert
quote *a search that is made*

through art-making does not have the
clarity of an ideogram unquote, a problem of

naming in relation to image
in the landscape or space, horizon erased

or transposed onto disembodied geometry's
bright techno-superstructure, so to ask

What is it? only a positive sign of lack
in the architecture's ultimate

immobility, the inertia of the material
groundmound. So then to desire

a general unframing, passage into the arc
of the kite, to get beyond the finality of

presets, to caress the air, as the difference
between material effects and material meanings.

All the singular figures
in motion, not touching, a pattern of trust

away from the broken authority
of the hierarchical, away from the one.

to Michael Ives

SONG OF THE *O* (EMERSON "CIRCLES")

O

horizon

forms   nowhere

copious

                 of forms.

One of now

admits of being outdone.

Our

no end in nature

a lower opens the moral fact

of the around.

Volatile.

             Our globe holds

snow

left in cold

         opens

for all that is old.

An old planet of the forgoing

                              the old roads.

You admire this tower, so

being narrowly lost

a gold mine or

more of the crop.

Moons are no more

bounds he obeys, be reformed

                showing

commands his own

                evolving circle

from a ring   larger circles, of circles,

will go   on the force

of the individual soul.

For having formed

a circular wave of a local usage, if the soul

                                over orbit

also outward a vast force

                       to disclose itself.

There is no outside, no inclosing

                how lo!

       on the other

a circle around the circle

outline.

To draw a circle outside

antagonist

as prophecies of its innocency

on the divine soul, otherwise.

The last closet was never opened: a residuum unknown.

Our moods do not   other

                                        a vast flow!

                        Choirs of his friends

game of idolatry   I know and worth

noble but

O!

We sell the thrones

a great hope, found his shores, found it a pond, Plato going

discordant

opinions we can never go

a conflagration has broken out, and no

man knows.

Valor

                        the power of self-recovery   so as

the magnet once a toy.

Poetry

      shows

efflux of goodness so   conversation

is a game of circles   conversation

bound the common of

stooping under the old

the cloven

flame glows on our walls

oppression, to oppress, to recover our

O   only

in orbs, the announcement

in common hours, society sits cold

knowing but prose and trivial toys

loomed so large in the fog's proportions

no words would be necessary no

a point outside

our hodiernal   circle

in Roman houses

diameter of the earth's orbit

the poet

in the encyclopedia   or the   or the   body

my old steps, and reform.

Ariosto writes me an ode   arouses

tones   my whole

open to the sides of all the solid old

lumber of the world

from a boat in the pond

against the dogmatism of bigots with this

word out of the book

of concentric circles   dislocations

manifold   other words explored

gravity of atoms

or the goods

      gravitate to you   also

omnipresence   of the soul behooves

he devotes a winged chariot

draws on his boots to go   through the woods lowest

to the verge of our orbit.

The poor and the low   be nothing

O broker no

though slower notes

does he owe

to be postponed

no virtue virtues of society.

The terror of reform

grosser moments that they abolish our   also

no longer reckon lost time no longer

poorly these moments

omnipotence

nothing of

O circular philosopher by beholding

into every hole

left open, my own and obey.

No facts

              no Past progression

the soul of circles   knowledge   contains all circles

no sleep, no pause

abhors the old and old age

only it by many forms of old age no

grow old, but grow to know

their hope organs of the Holy Ghost with hope

and this old age

the coming   only is sacred.

No love can be bound by oath

or covenant

no truth so.   People only

            any hope for them

total growths of the soul

I can know can have no guess for

so the sole

of so to know

the new position the powers of the old

moment all my once

hoarded knowledge to know—we do not know

the old and trodden round

a new road and better goals overpowering   or early cloud of so

of our propriety, without knowing

            how or of opium

                        oracular of the heart.

Ann Lauterbach was born and grew up in Manhattan, where she studied painting at the High School of Music and Art. She received her B.A. (English) from the University of Wisconsin (Madison) and went on to graduate work at Columbia University on a Woodrow Wilson Fellowship. She lived in London for seven years, working as an editor, teacher, and curator of literary events at the Institute of Contemporary Arts. Returning to New York, Lauterbach worked in art galleries for several years. She has taught in the writing programs at Brooklyn College, Columbia, Iowa, City College, and the Graduate Center of CUNY. Lauterbach has had residences at Yaddo, the Isabella Stewart Gardner Museum (Boston), the Wexner Museum (Columbus), and the Atlantic Center for the Arts (Orlando). She was a resident critic at the Anderson Ranch in Aspen and, from 2007 to 2011, was a visiting Core Critic (Sculpture) at the Yale School of Art. In 2013 she was named Distinguished Sherry Poet-in-Residence at the University of Chicago. Lauterbach has written essays on artists Joe Brainard, Ann Hamilton, Michael Gregory, and Cheyney Thompson and for the exhibition "Whole Fragment" at the Sheppard Fine Arts Gallery in Reno, Nevada.

Lauterbach has received fellowships from the Ingram Merrill Foundation, the Guggenheim Foundation, and the John D. and Catherine T. MacArthur Foundation. Her 2009 collection, *Or to Begin Again*, was a finalist for the National Book Award. She has been, since 1990, co-chair of Writing in the Milton Avery Graduate School of the Arts and, since 1997, David and Ruth Schwab Professor of Languages and Literature at Bard College. She lives in Germantown, New York.

JOHN ASHBERY
Selected Poems
Self-Portrait in a Convex Mirror

TED BERRIGAN
The Sonnets

LAUREN BERRY
The Lifting Dress

JOE BONOMO
Installations

PHILIP BOOTH
Selves

JULIANNE BUCHSBAUM
The Apothecary's Heir

JIM CARROLL
Fear of Dreaming:
    The Selected Poems
Living at the Movies
Void of Course

ALISON HAWTHORNE DEMING
Genius Loci
Rope

CARL DENNIS
Callings
New and Selected Poems 1974–2004
Practical Gods
Ranking the Wishes
Unknown Friends

DIANE DI PRIMA
Loba

STUART DISCHELL
Backwards Days
Dig Safe

STEPHEN DOBYNS
Velocities: New and Selected
    Poems, 1966–1992

EDWARD DORN
Way More West: New and
    Selected Poems

ROGER FANNING
The Middle Ages

ADAM FOULDS
The Broken Word

CARRIE FOUNTAIN
Burn Lake

AMY GERSTLER
Crown of Weeds: Poems
Dearest Creature
Ghost Girl
Medicine
Nerve Storm

EUGENE GLORIA
Drivers at the Short-Time Motel
Hoodlum Birds
My Favorite Warlord

DEBORA GREGER
By Herself
Desert Fathers, Uranium Daughters
God
Men, Women, and Ghosts
Western Art

TERRANCE HAYES
Hip Logic
Lighthead
Wind in a Box

NATHAN HOKS
The Narrow Circle

ROBERT HUNTER
Sentinel and Other Poems

MARY KARR
Viper Rum

WILLIAM KECKLER
Sanskrit of the Body

JACK KEROUAC
Book of Sketches
Book of Blues
Book of Haikus

JOANNA KLINK
Circadian
Raptus

JOANNE KYGER
As Ever: Selected Poems

ANN LAUTERBACH
Hum
If in Time: Selected Poems,
    1975–2000
On a Stair
Or to Begin Again
Under the Sign

CORINNE LEE
PYX

PHILLIS LEVIN
May Day
Mercury

WILLIAM LOGAN
Macbeth in Venice
Madame X
Strange Flesh
The Whispering Gallery

ADRIAN MATEJKA
The Big Smoke
Mixology

MICHAEL MCCLURE
Huge Dreams:
    San Francisco and Beat Poems

DAVID MELTZER
David's Copy:
    The Selected Poems of David
    Meltzer

ROBERT MORGAN
Terroir

CAROL MUSKE-DUKES
An Octave Above Thunder
Red Trousseau
Twin Cities

ALICE NOTLEY
Culture of One
The Descent of Alette
Disobedience
In the Pines
Mysteries of Small Houses

LAWRENCE RAAB
The History of Forgetting
Visible Signs: New and Selected
    Poems

BARBARA RAS
The Last Skin
One Hidden Stuff

MICHAEL ROBBINS
Alien vs. Predator

PATTIANN ROGERS
Generations
Holy Heathen Rhapsody
Wayfare

WILLIAM STOBB
Absentia
Nervous Systems

TRYFON TOLIDES
An Almost Pure Empty Walking

ANNE WALDMAN
Gossamurmur
Kill or Cure
Manatee/Humanity
Structure of the World Compared
    to a Bubble

JAMES WELCH
Riding the Earthboy 40

PHILIP WHALEN
Overtime: Selected Poems

ROBERT WRIGLEY
Anatomy of Melancholy and
    Other Poems
Beautiful Country
Earthly Meditations: New and
    Selected Poems
Lives of the Animals
Reign of Snakes

MARK YAKICH
The Importance of Peeling
    Potatoes in Ukraine
Unrelated Individuals Forming a
    Group Waiting to Cross

JOHN YAU
Borrowed Love Poems
Paradiso Diaspora